The Graduate's Guide to Grace in the Workplace

The Graduate's Guide to Grace in the Workplace

A Common-Sense Approach to Standing Out in Your Career

Anna Pikounis Paine

Paine Media Publications, Inc.

Published by Paine Media Publications, Inc., Jupiter, Florida
www.graduatesguide.com

Edited and designed by Girl Friday Productions
www.girlfridayproductions.com

Cover design: Emily Weigel
Project management: Abi Pollokoff
Editorial production: Kylee Hayes

ISBN (paperback): 979-8-9939747-0-5
ISBN (ebook): 979-8-9939747-1-2

Library of Congress Control Number: 2026903881

First edition

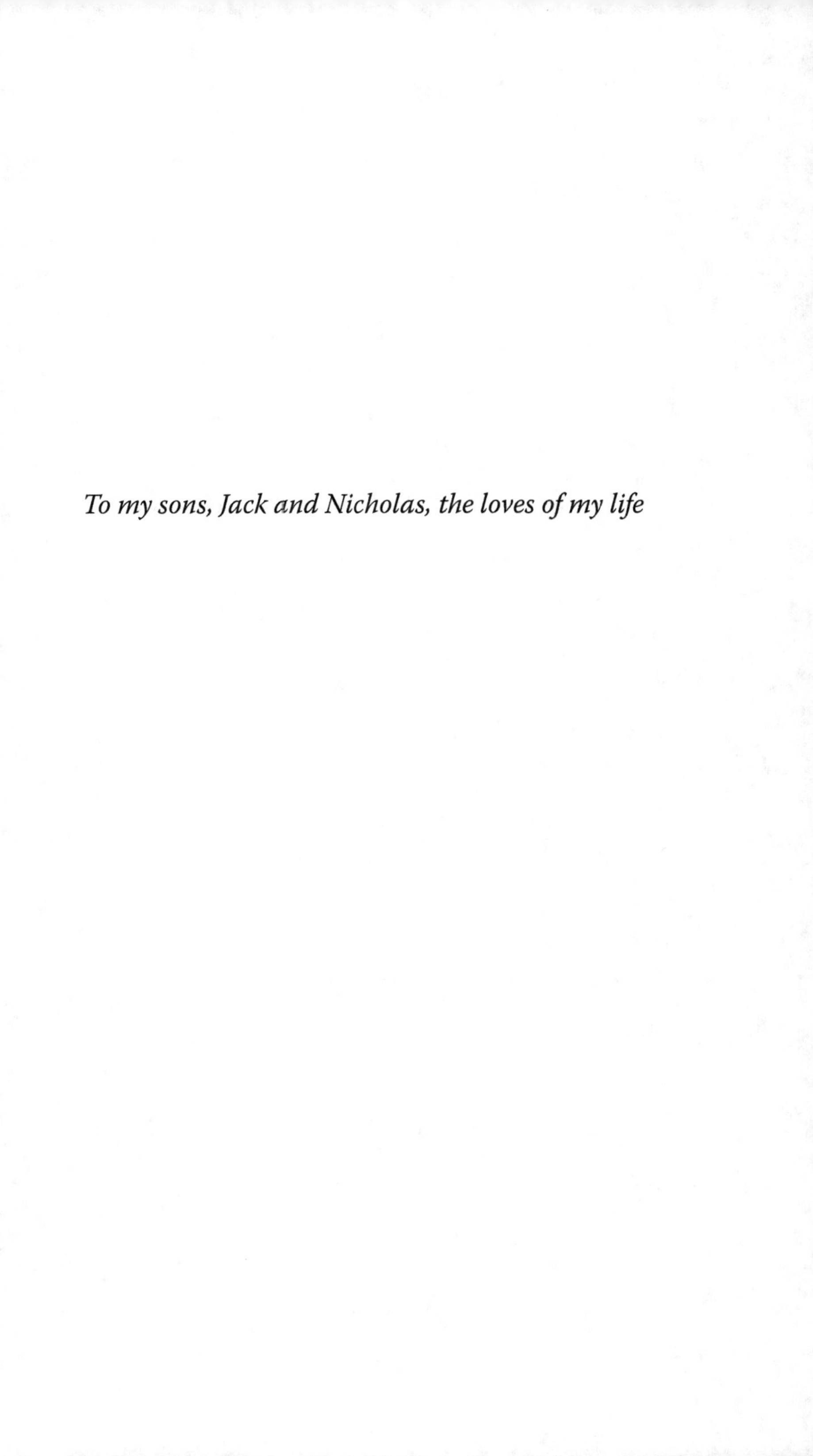

To my sons, Jack and Nicholas, the loves of my life

Contents

Letter to the Reader ix

Introduction 1

Part One: The First Impression

1. Make It Count 13
2. A Book *Is* Judged by Its Cover 19
3. Office Harmony 26
4. See No Evil, Hear No Evil, Speak No Evil 34
5. Grub, Gigs, and Grace 41

Part Two: The Next Impression

6. Become Indispensable 53
7. Talk Smart, Write Sharp 62
8. "Polite Confidence" Is the New PC 77

Part Three: The Last Impression

9. Leave in a Blaze of Glory 87

Author's Note 93
Notes 95
Acknowledgments 97
About the Author 99

Letter to the Reader

Dear Reader:

Thank you for reading *The Graduate's Guide to Grace in the Workplace.* I wrote this book in the hope of providing lessons and insights that I wish someone had shared with me when I was your age and just starting out in my new career. My goal is to make the beginning of your professional journey smoother and easier to navigate from the start.

Entering the workforce can feel intimidating. You are expected to know how to act, communicate, and present yourself before anyone has actually shown you how. This book is meant to bridge that gap. Through my real-world examples and honest advice, I hope to help you navigate those first few years. Whether you are beginning your first internship or stepping into your first full-time job, these pages are here to guide you toward becoming not just successful but respected, trusted, and indispensable.

But before we get started, you need to do some homework. I bet you thought you were done with homework forever! Well, this is a different kind of homework, which I will abbreviate as HMWK. This homework lays the foundation for all gracious workplace behavior discussed in this book. **HMWK** stands for **humility, manners, work ethic**, and **kindness**. A good dose of all will fill your soul and prepare you for what's ahead in your life. This foundation is crucial to your success in the workplace because it provides you with not only the awareness necessary to establish solid relationships with others but also a strong sense of self. Without this foundation, you will likely flounder in your new adult life, wondering why your coworkers respond to you the way they do, why it is difficult to make new friends, and why you don't feel so happy. I want you to focus on HMWK first so that you can successfully apply the advice provided in this book.

HMWK stands for humility, manners, work ethic, and kindness. A good dose of all will fill your soul and prepare you for what's ahead in your life.

The best way to start with HMWK is to stop and reflect on your life thus far. You can start with who raised you, whether it was a single mom, two parents, a grandmother, et cetera. Think about who these people are and how they positively shaped and also negatively affected your world. This may be one of the hardest things you will do in your life, because it will bring a flood of memories to the surface. Some of those memories will not be pleasant and may even bring tears to your eyes, while some will bring outright joy to your heart.

I recommend that you do this reflection now, as a young person starting your career, so that you can effectuate any behavior change necessary to move forward. God willing, you will have a long life ahead of you, and understanding who you are today, and who you really want to be going forward, requires this reflection. I experienced my reflection when I was starting my career, just like you are now. I would like very much to share my HMWK with you.

My HMWK

I was certainly raised to show humility, exhibit good manners, work hard, and be kind. A child of Greek immigrants, I grew up in a small house with a twin sister, older brother, and parakeets for pets. My parents worked in the kitchens of restaurants and fancy clubs in the area. The work required sweating, standing, and a lot of long hours, but they were always able to provide what we needed. We had a nice, clean home and good food on the table. We did not do the big clothes shop before the start of the school year. Neither my brother, sister, nor I was handed a car at the age of sixteen (or any other age for that matter). We all worked in high school for spending money, whether it was for pizza and a movie or a prom dress. We had to complete our chores before we were allowed to hang with our friends on Saturdays. We went to church almost every Sunday. My parents had very little extra money, so summer vacations were usually a three-day drive to my godparents' home in Baltimore for a family visit and back home again. The house rules and the consequences of breaking them were rough on us. The strict environment was suffocating at times. We did not have much, but we had enough. My parents did the best they could with what they knew. But quite frankly, like many young people, when the time came, I was ready to go away to college and leave this part of my life in the rearview mirror.

My parents had three children in college at the same time, so we qualified for financial aid. My brother, sister, and I never thought of our educations as an entitlement. Instead, it was a gift and a blessing that none of us took for granted. We all worked while in school, sometimes two jobs. Eventually, we all received degrees from the University of Florida.

Somewhere along the way I became a bit too enamored with myself and what I thought was a huge accomplishment. Here I was, a Greek girl from a town in which young ladies of my heritage did not go to college. They are typically married at the age of eighteen or so in somewhat arranged scenarios.

But I, Anna Pikounis, was pursuing a Bachelor of Science in Business Administration with a Major in Finance from the University of Florida at a time when business schools were male-dominated, and those women who did go to college were more drawn to traditionally female-oriented degrees, such as education, nursing, and liberal arts. Boy, I thought I was so smart and a real big deal.

Before I graduated, I interviewed with companies through the university's Career Resource Center and was offered a great job in the management-training program with the largest bank in Florida at the time, Barnett Bank. I was going to be a respected commercial loan officer, wear fancy suits, and work in a tall marble building in downtown Tampa! Now, I had *really* arrived and had no need for the simple, humble beginnings of my life. I thought, *Wow, look at me. I have accomplished this all on my own. I can live wherever I want, buy whatever I want, and make every single decision in my life without any influence from my parents ever again.*

After graduation, I moved to Tampa to begin my new life. I found a cute apartment with trendy mauve carpet (hey, it was the '80s), put a down payment on a used Chrysler LeBaron convertible, and bought some fancy suits from Burdines Department Store. I started working, as planned, and became immersed in the day-to-day monotony of waking up, getting ready for work, driving to work, working, driving home from work, eating dinner, watching a little TV, and starting the whole routine all over again the next day. Sure, I had been independent in college and had taken care of myself for years, but it was still only college. There were always so many fun things to do and people to see, and my schedule, despite being filled with classes and work, had some flexibility. And when I really wanted to, I could go home for the weekend and be pampered by my mom with a Greek dinner of roasted leg of lamb and spanakopita on Sunday before going back to my college life.

But this was it. This is what it really meant to work and be on my own in a new town with no family or friends. Just me and my big, fat "I have arrived" ego for comfort. I had a lot of time on my hands, which led me to the reflection I spoke of earlier. It was at this point that I began to realize that the foundation of everything I had accomplished thus far in my life was directly attributable to my parents.

My parents had been truly committed to raising three children and did not think of themselves while doing it. They did not belong to any fancy clubs. They saved every penny they could for college and retirement funds. The very few cars they owned were purchased with cash they had saved, and they kept those cars for ten to fifteen years. They did not have one credit card between them. They paid off their thirty-year mortgage in 1993 and never borrowed against the house. They raised us with solid morals and values. I'd never appreciated them or said thank you. This was an aha moment for me, and it changed my life.

In February 1990, about eight months after I had started working at the bank, I wrote a letter to my dad. It was his sixty-fourth birthday, and rather than just sending a birthday card, I wanted to express my gratitude for everything he and my mom had done for me and how much they had both played a part in who I'd become. It was true that I'd never taken the time to thank them—but I'd also never taken the time to forgive them. Remember, the reflection is for everything, the good and the bad. My good feelings about my parents far outweighed the bad, but it was important to acknowledge both. And then to move on from the bad.

Forgiveness gives you peace.

When I began writing this book, I asked my mom if she remembered the letter I'd written to my dad those many years ago. She not only remembered it; she had kept it.

The best way to start with HMWK is to stop and reflect on your life thus far. . . . Understanding who you are today, and who you really want to be going forward, requires this reflection.

Dear Dad,

Happy 64th, fats! How goes it in West Palm? Sorry your card is late, but you know how it is - being a busy business woman (ha ha)!

Things over here are going well. Work has been a little boring, but I think it will pick up soon. The bird is fine and learning a lot of things, including how to be mischievous!

Dad, the years have gone by quickly, but I just want you to know that everything I am today I owe totally to you and mom. You both were a little strict sometimes, but I'm finally at a point that I can look back and see why you did the things you did. I'm a good kid; we all are, because of you both. You were great parents and you will make wonderful grandparents in the coming years.

I miss home and you and mom and Nina. I don't miss yardwork (ha ha)! See you Friday Feb 23.

I ask you to set aside some time for your own reflection, and your own beginnings, before you continue reading this book. Now. You might want to go somewhere tranquil or stay in your quiet apartment. Maybe you decide to write in a journal or shout out to the entire universe. Whatever you do, be sure to take this time, and this step, seriously.

In addition to this reflection on your beginnings, I ask you for one more reflection. Take time to reflect on yourself. This will take some real honesty on your part. Do you embrace humility? Do you show good manners? Do you have a strong work ethic? Are you kind to others? I highly encourage you to pose these questions, and more, about how you show up for the people in your life, especially those whom you trust the most and who will give you an honest answer even when it hurts. The answers to these questions will enable you to forgive yourself, start over with a clean slate, and experience a brand-new beginning in your professional career and adult life.

Before proceeding with your career, strive to be at peace with yourself, with who you are, and with who you want to become.

Daily Life Lessons

You were likely taught at least some lessons about humility, manners, work ethic, and kindness throughout your life from parents, teachers, aunts, uncles, grandparents, and society in general. But have you actually *applied* those lessons in everyday life as well as you could? The good news is that you have the power to change that right now. This is the perfect time to choose the person you want to be and give yourself that clean slate by embracing these daily life lessons and the HMWK mindset as you enter the workplace.

☐ **Practice the Golden Rule: Do unto others as you would have done unto you.**
This simple thought is the foundation for all gracious behavior.

☐ **Recognize that you are 100% accountable for your actions.**
The blame game is not acceptable in a work setting. You are a grown-up, not an adult child. Take ownership of your mistakes by apologizing for them, learning from them, and not repeating them. You will be respected by your colleagues and boss for doing so.

☐ **Acknowledge that you are not the center of the universe.**
Almost nothing in the workplace will ever be solely about you. Check your ego at the door, and appreciate the opportunity you've been afforded.

☐ **Accept the fact that you are at the bottom of the organizational chart and be thankful you're even on the chart.**
Even the valedictorian of the most prestigious college in the United States will probably start at the bottom in a

new job. It is where you belong right now! But, of course, that will change with your effort.

☐ **Pay your dues with honor and grace.**
The idea that you can skip the hard work and garner quick payoffs is a fantasy. It's going to take a long time, but the hard work will pay off.

☐ **Listen more than you talk.**
Gathering good information by actively listening to others will result in better, more thoughtful processing and decision-making, and it will also go a long way to building relationships with others.

☐ **Commit to self-improvement every day.**
Be honest with yourself about your strengths and areas for improvement. If you're not sure what they are, ask someone who will tell you honestly and consider that knowledge a gift that you can use to improve yourself.

☐ **Emulate the behavior of people whom you truly respect.**
You will know very quickly who those people are by how they act in the office with coworkers, not by their contribution to the bottom line.

☐ **Maintain a positive mental attitude every day.**
The power of a positive attitude cannot be overstated! Your optimism, persistence, and self-belief will help you

influence outcomes. Also, a positive mental attitude is infectious and a magnet in the workplace for others to want to be around you and work with you.

Do unto others as you would have done unto you. This simple thought is the foundation for all gracious behavior.

Introduction

Congratulations! Whether you are graduating soon or have already graduated from high school, a trade school, a certification program, a training institute, or college, you achieved an academic goal you set for yourself, and you should be very proud. Your education will benefit your life in so many ways, but most importantly by providing you with the academic credentials necessary to find a job in your field and be financially independent. This independence is crucial to becoming your own person and forging your individual path for the rest of your life.

What You Didn't Learn in School

As you enter the workplace, you will apply what you learned from your education and other work experience. But were you ever offered a class on how to navigate workplace settings? This book is your go-to guide on professional workplace behavior.

Make no mistake. Your employer expects you to conduct yourself in a professional manner at all times from day one. They have the right to that expectation, and you should oblige. Understand right now that you are on *their* clock. Your behavior represents them, and you should always be mindful of this commitment. Professional behavior involves aligning with company values, portraying a positive professional image, and contributing to organizational success.

Professional behavior, like most behaviors, is not innate. As I presented earlier in the "Letter to the Reader," humility, manners, work ethic, and kindness (HMWK) are all integrated into professional workplace behavior, but we are born with none of them. We learn these behaviors from the people in our world and from society in general as we grow up. Ultimately, it is your responsibility to behave appropriately based on this knowledge, to determine the best methods to exhibit this behavior, and then apply those methods. This book provides the methods you can use in the professional setting.

Why Professional Behavior Is Critical to Your Success

Most of us will work 40+ hours per week, which means you are in the workplace approximately 40% of your awake time during the 40+ years of your career. Wow! That's a lot of time spent with people who are not your family or close friends. You want to ensure that your actions with coworkers contribute to respectful work relationships, which may even evolve into friendships.

You might be asking yourself, *Does the company really*

care how I act, as long as I work hard and increase its bottom line? Isn't my career advancement mainly based on my work performance? The answer is that both work performance *and* workplace behavior influence management decisions to advance your career. They are not mutually exclusive. The most significant difference between the two is that the evaluation of your work performance is typically much more objective, quantitative, and measurable, whereas the behavior component is mostly subjective. If you exhibit excellence in both areas, you will thrive.

Both work performance *and* workplace behavior influence management decisions to advance your career.

But let's be honest. As much as you want to thrive in your new career, you also simply want to keep your job. Job security can be very unpredictable. Throughout the first quarter of the twenty-first century, several significant events have proven this: the 2008 global financial crisis, the 2020 pandemic, and the emergence of artificial intelligence (AI), via large language models (LLMs) like ChatGPT, in 2022. Whether or not you were aware of, or remember, the details of the 2008 Great Recession, you or your family likely knew people who lost their jobs. The 2020 pandemic showed us how quickly the entire global economy can be shut down, through no fault of our own, and create widespread economic destruction. Currently, the global race for AI has placed enormous pressure on employers to implement it with the emphasis on reducing workforce or risk losing competitive advantage. These are extreme examples, but you get the point.

Even at a time when the economy is better, even thriving, you are never guaranteed your job. According to the US Department of Education, over four million students graduate from trade schools or colleges every year, which means competition for good jobs is always fierce.[1]

It's extremely important to develop a competitive advantage, which includes your job performance, certifications earned, and so on, but also includes how your level of professionalism is perceived by your superiors. *The Graduate's Guide* is here to help you with the latter.

What I Know About Professional Behavior

The Graduate's Guide is not yet another etiquette book written by a self-proclaimed expert on the subject. To my knowledge, no certification, license, or degree from a nationally accredited source exists for workplace etiquette, which is really just a fancy way of saying *good behavior*. While it can be defined in many ways, we know good behavior when we see it. We also know when we don't, and so do your boss and coworkers. So I will not use the "E" word in this book to describe good behavior. Let's call it what it is—common sense. Unfortunately, what constitutes common sense may not necessarily be common knowledge.

What makes the information in this book so useful is the source of information—my real-life experiences in the workplace for over thirty years. Once upon a time, I was you—one of the youngest employees in the company, just starting out, with very little idea of what to expect when I arrived at my new job. I've been a certified public accountant since 1994, with most of that time spent as the owner of my own firm and almost all my work performed at clients' offices. So from my early years at Deloitte, one of the Big Four accounting firms, where my job involved auditing public companies across the country, to my current work as an outsourced controller for small and midsize businesses, I've seen just about every kind of workplace: private investment firms, construction companies, bakeries, preschools, even an international music celebrity's office—you name it. And I have witnessed my share of questionable behavior among young professional staff. Sometimes it's a matter of poor judgment, like making personal calls from the work cubicle or showing up to work with wet hair. Other times, it's more serious, like being unprepared for meetings or missing deadlines. *The Graduate's Guide* is built to help you navigate all of it, wherever your career takes you.

Today, I am a workplace veteran who observes the younger versions of me in the work setting. Through many years of observation, I've determined that the questionable behavior of younger employees doesn't mean they are bad people or have no common sense. On the contrary, I've figured out that no one has probably ever taken the time to convey the general workplace behavior expectations to new staff. Oh sure, many companies offer impeccable training, comprehensive employee policies and procedures manuals, and step-by-step paths to company advancement, but no one talks about this other critical behavioral expectation. That's so unfortunate, because knowledge is power, and the lack of knowledge in this area can knock you down and out with no warning.

It's extremely important to develop a competitive advantage, which includes your job performance, certifications earned, and so on, but also includes how your level of professionalism is perceived by your superiors.

I am not an expert, nor do I need to be in order to pass on some good, friendly common-sense advice. Think of me as your Aunt Anna (not your mom), whom you love to spend time with at family dinners on Sunday because she always has some wisdom to share . . . and makes a mean Insta-worthy Greek pastitsio! My goal is not to lecture but to equip you with the tools and perspective I wish someone had shared with me. Take these lessons, apply them, and trust that they will serve you well. You'll make mistakes—everyone does—but you'll learn, adjust, and grow into the professional you aspire to be. One day, you'll be in the position to guide someone else just starting out. That is how strong careers, and strong professionals, are made.

How to Get Started

First, make sure you've read the "Letter to the Reader" and have spent some time on your reflection. Next, read the book in its entirety. Yes, the whole thing. You can do it!

Then go back, review one chapter each day, and practice the Daily Life Lessons described earlier for the first two weeks of your job. This is a good time to also practice applying HMWK regularly. Once these behaviors become second nature, you can then occasionally refer back to the book when you encounter bumps or anticipate new situations at work. For example, imagine your boss has just invited you to lunch with the team and you've got fifteen minutes to figure out how not to say or do something awkward. Flip to chapter 5, "Grub, Gigs, and Grace," for a quick dose of dos and don'ts, as well as confidence. You will walk in calm, cool, and totally lunch-ready.

The Graduate's Guide is written in a way to be informative and concise. After all, who has time to read a three-hundred-page book? You work now! The good news is that the book is just the right length—long enough to be jam-packed with good information but short enough to get through quickly.

It's also organized in three key sections to make it easy to start, stop, and retain. Part One, "The First Impression," explores how your appearance and personal workspace shape how others perceive you. This section is straightforward with brief bullets that are self-explanatory. Part Two, "The Next Impression," centers on your performance, reliability, and job security. This section is a bit more in-depth with more serious topics and recommendations. The final section, "The Last Impression," addresses the professional steps involved before and after leaving a job, and it warrants the same attention as all previous chapters, even if the advice is looking way into the future (we hope!).

Each section's chapters have an introduction to a specific topic followed by simple key points. That's it. This format allows you to read the entire book in great detail or simply touch on the key points of one chapter as a real-time refresher. I used this format because (1) I'm more of a "cut to the chase" technical writer, (2) you're smart enough to get the point without the fluff, and (3) we both have better things to do than to read (or write) unnecessary details. I guarantee you won't get bogged down by endless anecdotes or redundant explanations about how each concept relates to HMWK either. That said, I encourage you to research the many subjects in the book in greater depth based on your own work situation. Many of these subjects, such as appropriate attire, are workplace-specific, and no single book can cover them all.

The book is also written in broad terms, so its lessons apply to virtually any workplace from a centralized nursing station in a Los Angeles hospital emergency room to a construction trailer on a jobsite in Topeka, to an open stock-trading pit in New York, or even a Disney call-center cubicle in Orlando. Because no two workplaces are exactly alike, I vary the terminology throughout the book using words like *workplace, company, organization,* and *employer,* along with *boss, supervisor, colleague, peer,* and *coworker.*

Remember, this book is your go-to guide on professional workplace behavior. It is not meant to circumvent or supplant any policies established by your workplace. It's just some good common-sense advice from your Aunt Anna, and the goal is simple: Take the advice and adapt it to your own unique work environment.

Let's get started!

PART ONE

The First Impression

1

Make It Count

"You don't get a second chance to make a first impression." We have all heard that phrase, and it could not be more true. As you begin your career, move to another employer, or even start your own business, you will constantly meet new people and will want to present yourself in a polite, confident manner. That first impression can make a big difference.

One of my financial industry clients once asked me to take the lead in hiring four interns who could subsequently become full-time financial analysts for their firm. On the interns' first day, the firm's partners had a welcome breakfast in the conference room, at which time they greeted each intern as they entered the room and also spoke with them once everyone had sat down to eat. After the welcome breakfast, the interns moved on to their office space to begin the day with their immediate supervisors. What the interns didn't know was that, after the welcome breakfast, the partners remained in the conference room to discuss whom they would want to mentor based on the vibes of that first meeting.

I opened the partner discussion with the first name of one of the interns, and *all* the partners wanted to mentor that person. They jokingly competed against each other as to who should get the job, but the most interesting part of the jostling was *why* they were so drawn to that individual. In a nutshell, this intern had exuded confidence with a firm handshake, a sincere smile, and an impressive introduction as they sat for breakfast. Ultimately, the managing partner won the mentoring position, but the intern won even more, because this was about to become an opportunity of a lifetime that could not be matched if mentored by any of the other partners. After the internship, a full-time analyst position was offered, and, over the years, the intern was ultimately fast-tracked to partner.

"You don't get a second chance
to make a first impression."
. . . That first impression
can make a big difference.

☐ **A firm handshake with a sincere greeting is a must.**
The handshake is the first sign of confidence and professionalism during an introduction, along with a sincere "It's a pleasure to meet you." And please, no waving in lieu of the handshake when there are multiple introductions. Step forward, backward, around—whatever it takes to greet everyone with a handshake. Practice and perfect it. To this day, I love being told I have a great handshake.

☐ **Look people in their eyes.**
Nothing says you are listening and interested more than looking at a person's eyes when they are speaking. This is particularly important when you first meet someone. It is an immediate sign of respect.

☐ **Introduce yourself and others.**
If you're in a group setting and no one introduces you, take the initiative to introduce yourself. Likewise, if you're with someone who needs an introduction, take it upon yourself to do so, and try to also find some common topics to discuss to make the person feel comfortable and welcome. It's common courtesy. And it can also help build your own confidence.

> "Everyone, I'd like you to meet Jennifer. She just started with the firm in the tax practice. Jennifer, I'd like you to meet Ann, Rita, and Jack. Ann is also from Boston, your neck of the woods."

☐ **Be ready to briefly talk about yourself.**

At any moment, your boss or a colleague may ask you to tell a little bit about yourself, such as in a training session. Always have a practiced, up-to-date blurb to present to others to ensure that you sound confident and to avoid stumbling over your words. This is different from the interview question "Tell me about yourself" or the elevator pitch. You've already gotten the job, so the response is not related to your résumé. It should be a bit more personal.

> "Good morning. My name is Jennifer Smith, and I joined the company's accounting department about six months ago. I moved to Florida from Michigan. I'm really enjoying working with the team so far. And the warmer weather is really great, of course."

☐ **Use titles such as *Mr.* or *Ms.* to show respect.**

These titles can be especially meaningful when addressing older or high-level people until you have been told that such titles aren't required. When addressing a woman, use *Mrs.* only if you know she is married.

> Your boss, Joe Sanford, the seventy-one-year-old founding partner of your company, introduces you to his wife at the holiday party. "It's a pleasure to meet you, Mrs. Sanford" would be how you should reply. She will then let you know if you can call her by her first name.

☐ **Address people by their names.**

Addressing someone by name can help you to remember it. But more importantly, using their name can show you care, which is so important in today's world of impersonal connections. As Dale Carnegie, author of *How to Win Friends & Influence People,* wrote, a "person's name is to that person the sweetest and most important sound in any language."[2]

☐ **Smile.**

In a business setting, smiling demonstrates that you have confidence and creates a positive, professional atmosphere that encourages others to engage.

Key Points

First impressions play a powerful role in shaping professional relationships and opportunities, and they particularly reflect good manners, the *M* in HMWK. A confident handshake, genuine smile, direct eye contact, and respectful communication all signal professionalism and competence and often leave a positive, lasting impression that can open doors to career success.

2

A Book *Is* Judged by Its Cover

The book is you. The cover is your professional appearance.

Beauty is in the eye of the beholder, and so, too, is professional appearance. But what is professional appearance these days? When it comes to dress code, many employers have moved to "business casual," which is a bit of an oxymoron. Some have no stated dress code, so you're left to figure out on your own what attire is appropriate. Some jobs may not require a lot of interaction with customers, so you may think, *Why does it matter if I have a professional appearance?* Believe me: It matters. Your appearance is often a key factor in your success, so be cautious, and try not to confuse professional appearance with self-expression.

Your appearance is often a key factor in your success, so be cautious, and try not to confuse professional appearance with self-expression.

Your employer's cultural norms define what is "professional." Some employers want you to have a consistent professional image inside *and outside* their walls because consistency supports company branding and promotes a sense of teamwork, which can affect client perception. Admittedly, your personal style might conflict with your employer's intentions and, moreover, might be a distraction at work—but this is exactly the kind of attention you *don't* want. Employers have no obligation to allow you to dress, smell, or act however you want in the workplace or when representing the company beyond the company's walls. If this reality is not acceptable to you at your present job, then you might need to move on and find another if the "I am who I am" mentality isn't endorsed or even tolerated by your employer.

So then, what does it really mean to have a professional appearance in today's work setting? Because this topic is so broadly written about and varies by industry, I will ask you to do your own research along with prioritizing your employer's policies and observing your colleagues. What is expected at an international accounting firm in New York, a software company in California, a hospital in Michigan, or a car dealership in Texas will differ. Suffice it to say that how you dress and how you groom yourself are at the top of the list of considerations, and you should follow these basic principles regardless of industry or location.

Dressing

☐ **Do not wear wrinkled or dirty clothes.**
You are expected to maintain your wardrobe for work and have pride in your appearance, whether you're walking into your workplace or attending a virtual meeting, and regardless of whether you wear a uniform or select your own clothes. Either use a service to maintain your work clothes or spend a few hours each weekend washing and ironing the next week's wardrobe.

☐ **Always have at least one suit ready to wear.**
A ready-to-wear suit—pressed, clean, and coordinated with shoes and accessories—is an essential staple in the professional's closet. Even if there is zero chance you'll need a suit for work, it's a good idea to have one for other events (weddings, funerals, etc.) where your appearance could matter to your career, indirectly. You never know whom you will meet or what doors may open when you least expect it!

☐ **When in doubt, dress it up.**

You may attend various gatherings that require business attire. It is difficult to know what that means sometimes because of the shift to the ambiguous term *business casual*. If you hear or see these words, it means a suit. You will never be overdressed by wearing the expected suit, and you can always remove your jacket. You don't want to be the one who did not show up ready. You will look immature or unprepared, or as if you just don't care.

Grooming

☐ **Do not wear heavy colognes or perfumes.**

A light spritz or two is fine, but it is not appropriate to be drenched in the scent, which can actually cause allergic reactions in small spaces. At the very least, it can be annoying for the people who sit near you.

☐ **Brush, floss, and toss back the mouthwash.**

Few things are worse than having a conversation with your boss and seeing her step back for some odd reason (it's your breath). Brush your teeth before you come to work, after lunch, and anytime you sense that it's needed. Brushing your teeth is also a great pick-me-up in the middle of the day.

☐ **Don't come to work with wet hair or bedhead.**

Ladies, the wet hair suggestion is mainly for you, especially for those who have long hair, and the bedhead suggestion is mainly for the men, but the suggestions apply to both. When you come to work with wet hair or bedhead, you are immediately telling your boss that you're not prepared to start the day and that you don't think it's important to look professional at work.

☐ **Maintain clean nails (and toenails if open-toed shoes are acceptable in your workplace).**
Whether you get your nails done at a salon or use an inexpensive nail clipper, your hands are visible at work as you meet and speak with coworkers and clients. You don't need your nails to look fancy, just groomed.

☐ **Come to work clean-shaven.**
A clean-shaven face always presents well at the office. If you have a moustache or beard, trim it daily. You want to avoid looking scruffy like my husband when he goes surfing in the morning and skips the shave. Don't get me wrong—the scruff looks fantastic on him, but it's not appropriate for the work setting.

Expecting the Unexpected

☐ **Have an emergency stash of extra clothes at work.**
I know this may seem impossible given the small workspace you've likely been provided, but it's important to be prepared to change a blouse, your pants, or even underwear (yes, I said it) if something unexpected happens during work hours. You name it—it will happen! Simply

fold the clothes very flat and neatly with tissue papers and store in your desk, your locker, or any other space you may have. You'll be thankful you did.

☐ **Create a personalized goody bag with essentials and duplicates at work.**
The point of the goody bag is to hold items that you need at work or want to avoid having to leave work for. Here are some suggestions, mostly unisex, but y'all know the difference:

- Aspirin
- Makeup (second set)
- Feminine products
- Pepto-Bismol
- Tums
- Toothbrush/paste
- Floss
- Nail clipper
- Emery board
- Hand sanitizer
- Lip balm
- Razor
- Lotion
- Compact umbrella

Key Points

Your professional appearance is the "cover" of your personal brand, and it influences, whether directly or indirectly, how others perceive your competence, attitude, and even work ethic—the *W* in HMWK. Looking neat, clean, and prepared shows respect for yourself and your workplace. Dress appropriately for your industry, maintain good grooming habits, and be ready for unexpected situations with backup clothes and essentials. A consistent, polished appearance will build credibility and help you make a positive impression every day.

3

Office Harmony

As an entry-level employee, you will probably be given an entry-level workspace. It may be a cubicle with low walls, a desk in an open concept, or some combination of the two in tight quarters. The close proximity of large numbers of workers has its challenges, including seeing, hearing, and even smelling the actions of your neighbors. Your behavior at your desk, and around the common areas of the office, is yet another representation of you. Therefore, it is important to present yourself as an organized, clean, and responsible employee who comes to the office every day prepared to work.

Your first order of business is to read the policies and procedures in the employee manual. You will sign a document acknowledging you have read, and will follow, the material outlined. Some policies may seem very broad, unreasonable, and downright unfair. Well, that's just tough. Companies have every right to create their own standards, and any disregard for those standards can cost you your job and possibly getting the next one.

Some examples of common workplace policies that may lead to suspension or termination if ignored include disruptive behavior toward coworkers, customers, or management, using company equipment for personal activities, and spreading rumors that hurt company morale and reputation (see chapter 4). So follow the company handbook! You can't claim ignorance if you break a policy. And again, as stated in the introduction, none of the suggestions in *The Graduate's Guide* override anything specified in your employee handbook or by your boss.

In today's digital world, it is safe to assume that the company is monitoring your actions via security cameras, computer software, social media, and observation. You don't even need to know if they are, actually, but just assume, and behave accordingly.

Now, let's move on and discuss your behavior in and outside your workplace.

☐ **Maintain an organized workspace.**
Your boss and coworkers will walk by or come to your desk every day. Organization reflects a strong work ethic, so a disorganized, messy workspace can send the wrong message about you to your boss. Also, make sure you have all the supplies you need so that you don't have to ask your coworkers to use theirs.

☐ **Keep your hands off your coworkers' space and belongings.**
Don't use their desks, computers, or supplies just because it's convenient, without politely asking first. A person sitting close to the copier should not have her stapler used because it's on the closest desk to the copier. Go to your own desk and use your own supplies.

☐ **Eat your breakfast at home.**
You should not stroll into work and make a beeline to the kitchen to microwave your maple-flavored oatmeal cup, then eat at your desk. You should walk into work, sit down at your desk, and begin working. You are on company time. Show them you are ready to work every day the moment you walk in.

☐ **Eat away from your desk.**
If at all possible, eat anywhere but at your desk. The smell of the food and the noise from eating can be very distracting for others. Even if it smells good to you, it may not to your colleagues. More important, it is helpful to have a change of scenery from your desk to refresh yourself throughout the day. That said, eating at your desk is quite common and may even be expected, especially during crunch times, so always be aware of your surroundings and respect the senses of your close neighbors.

☐ **Be gentle when placing items on your desk.**
Because workspaces are sometimes connected or in

tight quarters, noise from each individual can be easily heard or felt. For example, if you receive a heavy box of work materials, gently place it on your desk, rather than just dropping it on your desk, which can be noisy and startle others.

☐ **Ask permission to interrupt your boss or colleagues during the workday with a question.**
Don't just walk up and start asking questions. Instead, knock on the office door or the cubicle opening and ask for the person's time with "Excuse me, may I speak to you for a moment?" It also works to send an advance email asking for the person's availability to speak with you about the topic, provided it is sent well in advance of your arrival at their door.

Companies have every right to create their own standards, and any disregard for those standards can cost you your job and possibly getting the next one.

☐ **Avoid ambushing people at work with your needs when they first walk in the door or when they're leaving for the day.**

Your own time management is crucial to your success, and your emergency issues or lack of planning should not become your supervisor's or coworkers' problem. Keep in mind that you're probably not the first person they plan to deal with when they come in to work in the morning. And while it may seem reasonable to wait until the day's end to approach them, as that avoids interrupting their plans for the day, it can also be perceived as rude to stop and ask for their help when they're getting ready to leave and go home to their personal lives. So be aware and find the proper time to approach.

☐ **Restrict communications from your desk to work-related matters only.**

If you need to make a personal phone call, email, or text, such as making a doctor's appointment or contacting a friend, make it elsewhere on your cell phone or from your personal email address during lunch or other breaks, away from your workspace. You're on the company's time when at work, and no one within earshot needs to know your personal business. If it's urgent, take a moment if you must, but in a private area. For work-related calls, do not use a speakerphone unless you're in a private room with the door closed and have asked permission to use it, so as not to disturb your coworkers.

In today's digital world,
it is safe to assume
that the company is
monitoring your actions
. . . behave accordingly.

☐ **Ignore your cell phone during your workday.**
Again, you are on the company's time and should not be checking texts, Instagram, sports apps, and the like. You can do all of that during breaks and lunch. If you know you are waiting for some important news, such as the results of your parent's medical test, let your supervisor know in advance so they understand why you are looking at your phone.

☐ **Offer to help others regardless of the task.**
Sometimes people will ask for your help, or you may see someone struggling with a task in the office. If you can help, you should. It may not be convenient for you or part of your established job responsibilities, but it reflects your positive attitude about your place in the office family. Also, if you complete your tasks ahead of schedule,

notify your boss and offer help where it's needed. This is the kind of initiative bosses remember.

☐ **Wash your hands.**

Almost everything can be heard in a bathroom and directly outside of it. Make sure you wash your hands after you use the bathroom to avoid grossing people out and spreading germs. No one wants to hear the toilet flush and see you walk out of the bathroom in three seconds. Ew!

☐ **Clean up after yourself, especially in a workplace kitchen.**

Your mama doesn't work there. Really.

☐ **End the day leaving a clean desk and a list of things to do the next day.**

Even when you're not in the office, your workspace reflects on you, so make sure it is clean and uncluttered, and be certain you are ready for tomorrow. Benjamin Franklin has often been credited with saying, "A place for everything, everything in its place."[3]

Key Points

Harmony in the workplace is a function of professionalism, respect, and cleanliness by all employees. Keeping your workspace organized, respecting others' workspaces, and reducing noise and smells are all key to projecting a responsible image. Perhaps more important, following company policies and assuming your actions at work are monitored are wise approaches to your daily behavior. Acting with consideration, discipline, and awareness in close quarters reflects your professionalism and exhibits both good manners and kindness—the *M* and *K* in HMWK.

4

See No Evil
Hear No Evil
Speak No Evil

We have all said and done things in our lives that we regret. While none of those errors in judgment may have gotten us fired from a job, one that could realistically lead to termination involves gossip or other forms of rumor-spreading. These can be considered forms of misconduct and a fireable offense, and even if participating in gossip doesn't get you fired, other consequences may ensue. Gossip signals immaturity and poor judgment on your part, which could lead your boss and colleagues to see you as unreliable and not focused on work. Moreover, gossip can poison a workplace atmosphere with mistrust, thereby reducing the positive morale and camaraderie necessary for smooth operations; in the end, gossip can irreparably damage professional and personal relationships.

Once, I was working at a client's office when the CEO called a company-wide meeting in the middle of the day. This was highly unusual, so needless to say, the employees were nervous about the content of such a meeting. The reason for the meeting was to inform everyone that a newly hired staff member had been fired and escorted out of the office immediately. (Some companies have a policy like this to ensure that employees do not return to their workspace, where they can sabotage or steal company assets, once they learn they are terminated.) The CEO openly explained that the newly hired employee had shared a rumor she'd overheard about a possible management shake-up. The story spread fast, and within days, it had reached the very manager she had mentioned. Though she hadn't meant any harm, the company viewed it as a breach of professionalism and trust as well as a disruption to the work environment.

Along with gossip, a host of other personal discussions and conversational styles do not belong in the workplace. Remember, these are not your family or friends. This doesn't mean you don't care about each other; it just means the workplace is for work. Now is a good time to assess how you interact with your coworkers to ensure you present a positive, respectful disposition with a focus on your work and not on the daily chatter around the proverbial water cooler. Often attributed to Socrates, there is a saying: "Strong minds discuss ideas; average minds discuss events; weak minds discuss people."[4] Regardless of its origin, the message holds timeless wisdom.

☐ **Never listen to gossip.**
Work gossip can be extremely damaging to company morale and coworker relationships. Eventually, the person who is gossiped about will find out you were part of the conversation, even if you only listened. Graciously and quickly step away from any sensitive conversation that even remotely sounds like gossip.

☐ **Never spread rumors.**
The workplace rumor mill is in constant flow about everything from coworker romances to imminent terminations. The only pertinent information you should be interested in at work is related to work and comes straight from the horse's mouth, like your boss. Staying above the fray shows integrity.

☐ **Never curse in the workplace.**
Cursing out loud is low-class and shows a true lack of professionalism. Granted, in some industries it may be commonplace, such as on a trading floor on Wall Street. However, just because you hear curse words from others around you, or use these words in your personal life, does not mean you should use them at work.

☐ **Never discuss controversial topics like sex, politics, or religion.**
It is inappropriate to discuss these topics in a workplace setting, even at a happy hour after work with your co-workers. Someone could become offended, and those feelings will find their way back to the workplace the next day. Save those discussions for trusted, personal relationships. Acceptable topics of conversation may include hobbies, travel, pets, sports, technology, fitness, and so forth. The list of topics is endless, so steer clear of controversial discussion points and politely change the subject as soon as possible if someone else is heading down that road.

Remember, these are not your family or friends. This doesn't mean you don't care about each other; it just means the workplace is for work.

☐ **Never discuss the big "news of the day" at work.**
Our lives are inundated with news 24/7 from cable networks and social media. I use the term "news" lightly, as most of the news stories are 10% fact and 90% opinion from so-called expert panels or followers in the comments section. We all have our own opinions, but the workplace is not the proper place to express them about topics unrelated to your work duties.

☐ **Never discuss personal matters at work.**
Keep your personal life separate from your work life. The fewer people who know about your personal problems, the better. As harsh as it may sound, you don't want to be known as the person at work who constantly shares personal issues or seeks sympathy from anyone who will listen. When a coworker asks, "How are you today?" it's simply a polite greeting, not an invitation to share your struggles.

☐ **Never tell stories about your party weekend or your dating escapades.**
This information about you is private, and your discussion or boasting about such stories may cause coworkers to quietly disrespect you.

☐ **Never complain about work or about coworkers to customers or other coworkers.**
Complaining, in general, signals negativity and lack of professionalism and can quickly label you as difficult to

work with. It can damage your reputation, your team's morale, and the organization's image. If you have a legitimate concern, address it privately with your supervisor and focus on finding a solution rather than venting frustrations.

☐ **Never confide in your coworkers regarding any of your alternative goals.**

"My *real* goal is to work for our competition." No! This is a perfect example of what *not* to say. Like a fire in a dry forest, this information will blaze through the company rumor mill and may negatively affect your path to promotion.

Key Points

Maintain your professionalism by avoiding gossip, rumors, personal matters, and controversial topics in the workplace. Although tempting, these types of conversations can harm reputations, damage trust, and even lead to termination. By staying above workplace chatter and focusing on work-related communication, you can strengthen your sense of humility—the *H* in HMWK—and protect both your credibility and your relationships from the negative consequences that often ensue from inappropriate talk.

5

Grub, Gigs, and Grace

You will attend mandatory work-related gatherings with colleagues, such as a department lunch or a training class. You will also receive invitations to coworkers' gatherings unrelated to work, or, on the other hand, you may not receive an invitation to a gathering while other coworkers did. Finally, you may be faced with an unexpected gathering void of invitations, such as the funeral of a colleague's parent. Gatherings with coworkers will be prevalent over many years of your career, and learning to navigate them with grace is essential.

One of my clients, a real estate development company, hired a young man as an assistant project manager. This was his first real job, and he was thrilled to be invited to a department lunch with his new boss and some of his coworkers on his first day. He wanted to fit in, so when others ordered cocktails, he followed suit.

Halfway through his oversized plate of pasta and two margaritas, he realized he'd said little while others chatted easily. He was a bit tipsy and tried to join in the conversation. He brought up a "funny" story about his college roommate's political views. Silence followed. His boss smiled politely and changed the subject to everyone's weekend plans. It was obvious to me that the boss had given him some grace because he was just starting out and did not want to embarrass him in front of the team by calling him out on the faux pas.

A few weeks later, the young man was left off the guest list for his boss's housewarming party. He felt hurt and wondered if the lack of an invitation was a dis related to that lunch with his coworkers and the inappropriate college-roommate story. But then he learned the party was limited to the company's partners and their families, who had all known each other for decades. Even though he, like most of his coworkers, was not invited to the party, he sent a short note congratulating his boss and wife on their new home. The next week, his boss invited him to a small business-networking event, saying, "I really appreciated your kind note."

The young man learned two important lessons: Work gatherings are still work, and good manners are never wasted.

Gatherings with coworkers will be prevalent over many years of your career, and learning to navigate them with grace is essential.

Eat, Drink, and Be Merry-ish

☐ **Keep in mind one overarching thought: Your coworkers are not your family or friends.**
During gatherings, you're still on the job, and professional behavior still applies. However, these gatherings are an opportunity to build relationships with all participants, so approach them with enthusiasm.

☐ **Maintain an air of professionalism even outside the office.**
Choose foods that are neat and easy to eat. Avoid anything messy, overly heavy, or likely to cause stomach discomfort later—especially while you're still at the event.

Limit or skip alcohol entirely, depending on the occasion.

Resist ordering the most expensive item on the menu, no matter what others choose. The goal is to enjoy the event, not to draw attention to yourself or your plate.

☐ **Strive to keep conversations balanced and inclusive so everyone feels part of the discussion.**
Encourage quieter colleagues to join in by asking friendly, open-ended questions.

☐ **Be mindful not to dominate the conversation.**
Avoid sensitive topics like politics, religion, sex, or personal matters. Keeping the tone light and professional ensures a pleasant atmosphere for everyone.

☐ **Bring the host a gift if you attend a gathering unrelated to work, such as a holiday party at your boss's home.**
The gift need not be expensive and should not be too personal. Typical host gifts are chocolates, wine, flowers, or a candle. If you know the host fancies something specific, such as a special brand of international coffee, that's even better.

The purpose of this gift is to serve as a gesture of gratitude for the invitation and hospitality. Of course, you still must always thank the host in person as you depart.

Invitations and Expectations

☐ **Always RSVP.**

RSVP is an acronym for *Répondez s'il vous plaît,* which quite simply means "Please respond." Never assume the host *knows* you'll be there. Most gatherings require a good head count, and hosts are too busy making all the plans to follow up with guests or guess their intentions. It's downright rude to *not* RSVP, regardless of whether the event is work-related or personal.

Respond timely and in writing to every invitation you receive by mail, email, phone message, or text. The requested form of your reply will often be indicated in the invitation.

If you RSVP'd that you *would* attend, and then cannot for some reason, let the host know before the gathering that you have changed your plans.

Work gatherings
are still work,
and good manners
are never wasted.

☐ **Be especially careful regarding personal events hosted by your coworkers.**
If you receive an invitation to a coworker's event, such as a wedding or a birthday party, make sure you RSVP. In addition, bring a gift, dress appropriately, and follow the "Eat, drink, and be merry-ish" suggestions.

> It's OK to decline an invitation; after all, you have a life. But generally speaking, it is best to attend whenever you can. It shows respect to your coworker, who also showed you respect with an invitation.

☐ **Let it go if you don't receive an invitation.**
Hosts must make hard decisions regarding the size of an event and related costs, what makes the most sense, and whether their guests will feel obligated to bring a gift. For example, your boss may host her eight-year old's birthday party on a Saturday afternoon at a local pizza arcade and only invite those coworkers with children of a similar age. It wouldn't make sense to invite you, a twenty-three-year-old single guy with no kids, as that may put pressure on you to attend and/or purchase a gift. So give the host the benefit of the doubt if you're not invited.

☐ **Recognize that funerals are special circumstances.**
Death is not convenient, and no one wants to attend a funeral, especially if they've never even met the deceased.

But here's the kicker: The funeral is for those left behind. A funeral serves as a way to gather one last time to remember the deceased and have closure so that the real grieving can begin. The one left behind, your coworker, needs all the support they can get.

> Gatherings for a death also include wakes, celebrations of life, formal religious services, graveside burials, and so forth. You need not attend all, just pick one and go. The beach day, the football game on TV, and any other plans you would rather make will still be there another time, but this is a one-shot chance to show your respect and grace to your coworker, who, in turn, will be grateful that you took the time to attend. If you absolutely can't attend any of the gatherings, always send a sympathy card and donate, even a small amount, to any cause listed in the obituary, which can easily be found online.

☐ **Send thank-you notes.**

Thank-you notes are a time-honored tradition and should be used as much as possible in a business setting. Make it a point to purchase personalized stationery with your name embossed and always have a stamped envelope ready. Send the note to the recipient within two to three days after the gathering or event. The note should be short, specific, and personalized.

Here are some quick thank-you-note templates you could send to a host or event organizer.

> *Dear Anna,*
>
> *Thank you for hosting such a beautiful holiday party at your home. The food and music were terrific, and I especially loved meeting Max. What a sweet dog! Everyone had a great time, and I hope to see you again soon.*
>
> *Sincerely,*
> *James Smith*

> *Dear Anna,*
>
> *Thank you for organizing the business retreat at the Hyatt Regency Lake Tahoe. I greatly appreciated the opportunity to connect with my colleagues from around the country and to hear about the future plans for the company. I feel honored to be part of such a fantastic team.*
>
> *Sincerely,*
> *James Smith*

Key Points

Every social or professional gathering with coworkers, whether a business lunch, happy hour, or personal event, is still an extension of the workplace, and as such, how you handle it will affect your reputation. Professionalism should always be on your mind: Eat neatly, drink modestly, engage in balanced conversations, and avoid controversial topics.

Always RSVP promptly, bring an appropriate host gift for private gatherings, and show appreciation with thank-you notes afterward. If you aren't invited to an event, don't take it personally, because hosts make difficult choices. Even somber occasions like funerals offer an opportunity to show empathy and support for colleagues, which leaves a lasting impression of grace and respect.

While external events may seem peripheral to your job, they actually give you the opportunity to demonstrate humility, good manners, work ethic, and kindness—the full wingspan of HMWK.

PART TWO

The Next Impression

6

Become Indispensable

You are expected to perform at the highest professional level in order for the company to meet or even exceed its goals. You will complete numerous daily tasks, attend an endless number of meetings, and report to management on an ongoing basis to make sure you understand your role in the company and are on the path to achieve your delegated goals. Your boss regularly communicates these quantitative goals to you.

One of your key goals must be to make yourself indispensable. The benefits of being indispensable may include high raises, frequent promotions, and great respect from your clients and colleagues. It may also save you from termination due to layoffs. How on earth can you become indispensable when you're on the bottom of the organizational chart? You start on *day one* and never stop.

I started my CPA firm in 1996 without a single client after leaving Deloitte, where most of my work involved auditing public companies. In order to build my practice from scratch, I needed client referrals from colleagues, friends, and family. This was actually the easy part since I lived in my hometown and already knew a lot of people. The hard part was making sure *from day one* that I performed at the highest level and made myself indispensable to my clients. If I were to achieve that goal, the referrals would be never-ending, and I could go on to have a successful business for the next thirty-plus years . . . and that's exactly what happened.

I've had one client in particular since 2011 who's been the best client of my entire career. He's in his seventies now and works every day because he genuinely loves what he does. Over the years (hopefully many more to come), I've made myself indispensable to him by providing impeccable service and implementing the many suggestions from "The Next Impression." I'm always available to discuss his business, any time of day, any day of the week, and from any location. He often uses me as a sounding board for ideas, values my input, and regularly asks for options, followed by my recommendation. I've also spearheaded many complex projects on his behalf, coordinating with outside attorneys, bankers, and the like to ensure every detail aligns with his goals. And last but not least, I meet deadlines—every time. It's one of the simplest yet most powerful ways to earn trust and prove reliability.

Beyond my technical performance, I also bring a positive

attitude to every interaction, whether walking through his office door or answering his call, by greeting him with a genuine smile and upbeat energy. When those times arise that I disagree with him, I respectfully share my honest opinion in a calm and professional tone, and he knows he can trust me. I have shared in both his joyful and difficult moments over the years, attending celebrations and funerals for people close to him. What began as a standard client engagement has evolved into a trusted partnership and friendship built on mutual respect.

Becoming indispensable in your career involves more than a solid performance of your job. It involves professional and gracious behavior, in part because you represent the organization at all times and also because people naturally want to work with others whom they respect and like to be around. Make your gracious behavior a daily priority.

☐ **Demonstrate reliability.**
As you are assigned goals and tasks, you must complete them consistently with a high level of quality and reliability, and always on time, sometimes under enormous pressure. Every time you deliver strong results, you reinforce your boss's confidence in your abilities. In the long run, that reliability builds trust, making you someone your supervisor can count on as an invaluable asset to the team. This earned trust not only enhances your reputation but also increases your job security and positions you for future growth and promotion.

☐ **Figure it out by being resourceful.**

You are now an adult with an education and a new career. You must act like it and learn not to rely on others unnecessarily. No one is going to hold your hand in the work environment. Being resourceful is expected, but it's not usually communicated by management so directly. A resourceful person is one who takes initiative, tries new approaches, adapts quickly to plan changes, thinks critically to solve problems, and makes the most of available resources. Combining these elements leads to more efficient and effective outcomes, adding to your successes.

☐ **Build your credentials and your cred.**

You will need to determine the additional training, skills, or certifications you can proactively pursue to become a star in the eyes of your boss. Taking initiative to strengthen your expertise and staying current in your field with credentials will signal ambition and commitment. You should also build cred by taking the initiative to volunteer for a project or propose a project of your own *specific to* the organization, even if there is no hard credential awarded. When you complete additional work, update your résumé and professional profile in real time, and make sure your boss is aware of your continuous pursuit to improve yourself with the company in mind. Of course, updating your résumé will also keep it current in the event a job change becomes warranted.

One of your key goals must be to make yourself indispensable. . . . start on *day one* and never stop.

☐ **Embrace technology.**
Technology is a part of almost every industry. Proactively learn and use all the technology available at your workplace, regardless of whether your peers or colleagues choose to do so. Pay particularly close attention to AI, which is changing almost every field. The people who learn how to effectively use it early will have a serious edge in the workplace. The real threat isn't always that AI will replace your job, but it might *take* your job if your coworker knows how to use it and you don't. AI can summarize reports, organize data, and even brainstorm ideas when you're stuck. It also often allows you to finish tasks faster, thereby freeing up time for other projects and making you look like the person who always knows how to get things done. Whenever you use technology to make everyone's job easier, you stop being "just another employee" and start becoming the one your boss cannot imagine losing.

☐ **Be prepared for every meeting.**

Your boss may call you into their office, stop by your desk, or electronically summon you to a meeting in the conference room to discuss a task, and you should always have a notes app (if allowed by your boss) or notepad available to jot down the exact instructions. After your boss is done speaking, repeat those instructions back, and always ask for an expected time of completion if not already conveyed. This way, you can prioritize the request among all your tasks and projects, demonstrate that you show attention to detail, and prevent mistakes due to a lack of communication. Being prepared for every meeting will confirm that you should become your boss's go-to person.

☐ **Smile and greet everyone from the janitor to the CEO.**

Courteous behavior is expected in our society's workplaces, although it can be in short supply at times. Smiling and greeting everyone builds relationships and trust across all levels in the workplace, and people naturally want to work with those who make them feel valued and respected. Your friendly and respectful reputation will also help keep your name at the top of people's minds when opportunities arise. Don't just smile at the people higher on the organization chart; the CEO's father may have been a blue-collar worker like a janitor (or a waiter, like my dad).

☐ **Be a team player.**
You will be given opportunities to work in group settings to accomplish a goal. Employ the mindset of ac-
complishing the goal by respectfully listening to the
ideas of others and then also presenting your own. Do
not ever embarrass a coworker by knocking their idea
in a negative way. Instead, tactfully express the reasons
you don't agree and graciously present your own (more
on this point in chapter 7 re: the Google study). Being a
team player makes you indispensable because it shows
that you care about the company's success, not just your
own, and managers quickly recognize employees who
unite rather than divide a team. Those are the people
they trust to lead projects, resolve conflicts, and represent the company with grace.

☐ **Ditch the balance and do the work.**
As a new employee, your reliability and willingness to go
above and beyond will define your reputation. Arriving
on time, staying the full day, and being available outside
normal business hours shows commitment and respect
for your job. Working hard while you're young, and have
fewer responsibilities, also lays the foundation for future
work-life balance and even early financial freedom. If
your boss knows you can be counted on to show up, stay
engaged, and handle any task, you will be seen as invaluable. This takes conscious awareness and a lot of work,
but if you commit to it, you will reap the rewards.

Make your gracious behavior a daily priority.

- ☐ **Ask for constructive criticism and thank your boss for it.**
  Take the criticism positively, no matter how harsh it feels. This is one of the hardest things to do, but also one of the most mature and valuable behaviors you can demonstrate early in your career. Feedback is how you improve faster than your peers, so listen carefully, take notes, and show visible effort to make changes. When you welcome correction instead of resisting it, your boss sees that you are coachable, resilient, and focused on growth, making you an employee your boss wants to invest in.

- ☐ **Avoid the "that's not my job" mentality.**
  If your boss asks, it *is* your job. Early in your career, you are not just being paid for the tasks listed in your job description. You are paid to solve problems and make your boss's life easier. The most successful employees are the ones who step up, take initiative, and handle whatever needs to get done without complaint or hesitation. Every time you say yes and deliver results, you build trust, expand your skill set, and become the person your boss knows can handle anything.

Key Points

A primary career goal should be to make yourself indispensable—someone your boss, team, and clients can't imagine losing. Through exceptional performance, reliability, and professionalism, you can set yourself apart, and this may lead to raises, promotions, and job security even during layoffs. Being indispensable is not about status or title. It is about performance, professionalism, and grace that make others respect and depend on you, and it draws upon the full spectrum of HMWK's components.

7

Talk Smart, Write Sharp

Your ability to communicate will make a significant difference in the success of your career. A good communicator conveys a clear message that contains the information the receiver needs and is delivered in a manner in which the receiver understands. Albert Einstein is widely credited with saying, "If you can't explain it simply, you don't understand it."[5] Let these words become your guiding principle.

In the workplace, communications in any form should follow basic principles to ensure the company runs like a well-oiled machine. The seven *C*'s of communication are a "set of principles for effective communication" first introduced in the book *Effective Public Relations*, in 1952.[6] These principles are just as applicable today.

1. **Clear:** The purpose and intent of your message should be unambiguous. Avoid jargon and minimize the number of ideas in each sentence to make it easy for your audience to understand.

2. **Concise:** Get to the point quickly and efficiently. Eliminate unnecessary words, sentences, and repetitions to save your audience time and keep them focused on the core message.

3. **Concrete:** Use specific details, facts, and figures to make your message solid and vivid. Concrete communication leaves no room for misinterpretation and adds credibility.

4. **Correct:** All communication should be accurate and error-free. This includes checking for grammatical errors, correct spelling, proper formatting, and factual accuracy.

5. **Coherent:** Ensure your message is logical, well organized, and easy to follow. All points should be connected and relevant to the main topic, with a consistent tone and flow.

6. **Complete:** Provide your audience with all the necessary information. A complete message includes all relevant contact information, dates, times, and a clear call to action if needed.

7. **Courteous:** Be friendly, open, and honest. Show respect for your audience by considering their viewpoint and needs. A courteous tone helps build rapport and prevents miscommunication.

Keeping these principles in mind, let's move on to the three types of communication—verbal, nonverbal, and written—and the most *common* mistakes I consistently see among young professionals. If you fix these, you're most of the way home.

Verbal

Speaking can be one of the most frightening experiences for young professionals, whether it be a one-on-one conversation with the boss or a presentation in front of an audience. In my experience, the most important of the seven C's for successful spoken communications but the least observed among young professionals is the first one: *Be clear.*

- Unambiguous purpose and intent.
- No (or limited) jargon.
- Minimized number of ideas in each sentence.

Lack of clarity leads not only to confusion but also to a lack of credibility, which is a crucial component to earning the respect of your peers, your boss, and your clients.

One of the most common speaking mistakes is weaving unnecessary words and phrases into your sentences, such as *like, you know, I think, I mean, kinda, sorta,* and *right.* Weaving makes your message unclear and makes you sound ill-prepared, immature, and unsure of yourself. Similarly, ending sentences with the tone of asking a question makes your statements sound weak, as if you have no confidence in what you just said. Unfortunately, this way of speaking is prevalent in everyday conversations and heard constantly in media.

Below are two statements, one with "weave" and one without. Imagine your supervisor asked why Netflix subscriptions declined in the second quarter among the eighteen- to twenty-nine-year-old age group. Which response sounds more credible?

1. Sales of Netflix subscriptions for eighteen- to twenty-nine-year-olds declined 19.5% in the second quarter of 2025 due to lower customer demand, caused primarily by employees returning to work in the office.

2. Um, well, I mean, sales of Netflix subscriptions for eighteen- to twenty-nine-year-olds sorta declined 19.5% in the second quarter of 2025 kinda due to lower customer demand caused primarily by, you know, employees returning to work in the office, right?

The most important of the seven *C*'s for successful spoken communications . . . is the first one: *Be clear.*

OK, it's an exaggeration, but you get the point. Be honest with yourself. Do you regularly speak like the second responder? You wouldn't write statement no. 2 in a report, so why would you state the same fact in that manner when speaking? The goal is to speak precisely, properly, and professionally.

Are you always going to speak perfectly? No, and that's OK, as long as you sound credible 95% of the time. Practice the craft of proper speaking every day, whether you're speaking to your boss or to your best friend. Over time, your speaking skills will improve, your credibility will increase, and your confidence will soar.

Nonverbal

Nonverbal communication is just as important as verbal, maybe even more so. Nonverbal communication can include facial expressions, eye contact, and gestures, but the most important nonverbal communication is listening. The good listener is communicating respect to others, which strengthens relationships and builds trust, all crucial elements of workplace success. Since you will likely spend a good portion of your time in group settings in your workplace, let's talk about the deep connection between effective teams and listening behavior.

Companies rely on teams to accomplish goals that are too complex or wide-ranging for individuals to achieve alone. By grouping employees with diverse skills and perspectives, teams can approach problems more creatively and make better decisions. When teams function well, they foster a sense of belonging and shared purpose, which boosts morale and retention. In short, teams are the backbone of most modern organizations: They enable companies to operate efficiently, adapt to change, and stay competitive in a fast-moving business world.

One of the largest and most successful companies in the world actually studied their teams to determine why some were more successful than others. Google's internal company study, Project Aristotle, concluded that "psychological safety" was the strongest predictor of team success by how it drives innovation, performance, and retention.

> *Psychological safety: A strong team culture was correlated with each member's perception of the consequences of taking an interpersonal risk. Those on teams with strong cultures feel safe taking risks in the face of being seen as ignorant, incompetent, negative, or disruptive. In a team with high psychological safety, teammates feel safe to take risks around their team members. They feel confident that no one on the team will embarrass or punish anyone else for admitting a mistake, asking a question, or offering a new idea.*[7]

Team performance and listening skills are deeply connected because successful teamwork depends on trust, understanding, and respect, all of which are communicated as much through body language and active listening as through words. In a team setting, listening signals attentiveness and genuine interest in others' ideas, encourages participation, and makes team members feel valued and heard. When people feel listened to, they're more likely to share ideas, resolve conflicts productively, and collaborate effectively. Listening strengthens the human connection that turns a group of individuals into a cohesive, high-performing team.

The most important nonverbal communication is listening.

- ☐ **Listen to build a foundation of safety.**
  When team members feel genuinely heard and their opinions are not dismissed, interrupted, or ignored, they begin to trust that speaking up won't lead to embarrassment or punishment. This sense of *being valued* is the heart of psychological safety. Active listening (eye contact, paraphrasing, nodding, and asking clarifying questions) communicates respect and openness.

- ☐ **Encourage voice and reduce fear.**
  Psychological safety means people believe they can take interpersonal risks, such as admitting mistakes or challenging an idea, without negative consequences. When others *listen thoughtfully* instead of reacting defensively,

it reinforces that belief. Over time, listening builds a culture where people feel safe to contribute creative or dissenting ideas.

☐ **Thrive with positivity and trust.**
Listening and safety create a positive cycle: The more people listen, the safer others feel; the safer they feel, the more openly they share. This improves collaboration, problem-solving, and team innovation, exactly what Google's Project Aristotle identified as the mark of high-performing teams.

Listening attentively and allowing others to express their ideas helps create a psychologically safe environment, one where people feel comfortable taking risks, asking questions, and speaking up without fear of embarrassment or judgment. You have two ears and one mouth for a reason.

Written

Written communication is essential in the workplace because it ensures clarity, professionalism, and consistency. It also provides a permanent record of information and helps teams stay productive. Written communication comes in many forms such as memos, reports, and instant messaging and online chat (e.g., Slack, Microsoft Teams). I will focus on emails specifically because they are currently the most generally accepted and commonly used form of written communication in the workplace.

Let's first talk about general email courtesy and structure.

☐ **Give a reasonable deadline for a reply.**
Your colleagues are prioritizing work tasks all day long, and you may not be their priority. You can help them know how important a timely response is by letting them know clearly in your email. But be careful: Emails denoted as urgent and high-priority should be rare. Your job is to be patient and give ample time to your recipients whenever possible.

☐ **Stay where you are.**
Although you might be tempted to walk over to a co-worker and say, "I just emailed you about ___________," this behavior misses the point of emails. Allow your colleagues to remain focused on their task at hand and to use their own skills and processes to continuously and efficiently prioritize new written requests without interruption.

☐ **Avoid email war.**
Regardless of how combative an email in your inbox might seem, don't engage in "war" with anyone through email. The war will never end, and the proof of that war—and the words used—are permanent. A short, courteous response is the best way to go. "I understand your concerns. Let's set up a time to discuss the issues."

☐ **Follow up important verbal discussions.**

One of the best ways to use email is to summarize and memorialize in-person discussions and meetings. This practice used to be accomplished with written or typed memos, and memoranda may still be used in your organization. But nowadays, emails are usually preferred as a quick way of documenting what was said, agreed to, actions required, et cetera. Emails also ensure that everyone has the opportunity to ask for clarification on a given matter so that ultimately the entire team winds up on the same page.

☐ **Let people rest on the weekends, holidays, and their days off.**

If you're working on the weekend, good for you! But don't send emails to your boss or coworkers over the weekend if the matter can wait. You wouldn't call them over the weekend unnecessarily, and even though emails are not the same as a phone call, almost everyone receives work emails on their phone with a notification sound, so it's still an interruption of their personal time.

☐ **Use a professional font.**

Times New Roman or Garamond and a point size of 11 or 12 are standard and acceptable fonts. Limit under-lining, bold, italics, and color-coding; never use ALL CAPS; and refrain from using emojis, images, or other unprofessional inserts.

Now let's talk about basic email content.

- *Address lines:* Using the correct "To," "Cc," and "Bcc" fields helps everyone quickly see what's expected of them, prioritize their tasks, and respond without confusion or wasted time.

  > "To"—The main people you're addressing who are expected to read and take action on the message or are directly involved in the topic.

  > "Cc"—The people who need to be informed but aren't required to act. The carbon copy is used more sparingly than "To."

  > "Bcc"—People who receive the message without others knowing they did. The blind carbon copy is very rare and can be considered sneaky by some, so, quite frankly, I recommend not using it at all.

- *Subject line:* Summarize the email's purpose in concise, specific language. You may also add "Pls. reply" to the beginning of the subject line so recipients know a reply is needed.
- *Opening salutation:* Use a professional salutation, such as "Dear Jim" or "Hi, Jim" (if it's appropriate to be so familiar with Jim).

> # Written communication is essential in the workplace because it ensures clarity, professionalism, and consistency. It also provides a permanent record of information.

- *Body:* Write concise and to-the-point content for the purpose of the email and any next steps, including requests or deadlines. Keep the seven C's in mind.
- *Closing salutation:* Use a professional closing salutation, such as "Thank you" or "Sincerely."
- *Signature:* Include your name, title, and contact information along with company logo and any required disclaimers.

Always keep in mind that your colleagues' and customers' time is valuable and limited. Many people who open a lengthy email will close it immediately, with the intent to read it later, but that may end up being never. Follow these basic email recommendations and you can feel assured that your email will be opened, read, and addressed.

Before closing, let me add a note about emails and AI.

Artificial intelligence has revolutionized email writing by making communication faster, clearer, and more professional. AI tools use natural language processing to suggest wording, correct grammar, adjust tone, and summarize long email threads, all of which allows the employee to focus on content and strategy rather than mechanics. However, over-reliance on automation can make emails sound robotic. A good approach is to use AI to assist with your email structure and clarity, while ensuring your final message reflects your authentic voice and professionalism. Write like the professional human that you are, not like a polite robot.

Key Points

Embracing the seven *C*'s will help you master your communication skills, build confidence, and establish credibility: Be clear, concise, concrete, correct, coherent, complete, and courteous.

Practice your verbal skills every day, and avoid weaving fillers into your sentences such as *you know, like, I mean,* and *sorta.*

Strong nonverbal skills—eye contact, posture, facial expressions, and especially listening—build trust and respect faster than any title on your business card. Active listening is especially critical as it creates psychological safety and turns good teams into great ones.

Writing skills are critical because written documentation, including email, is where professionalism meets permanence. Make it count, and help your recipients manage their response. Avoid unprofessional content (such as emojis) and email warfare.

Always proofread before hitting Send, and learn to use AI tools to build and polish your message, but don't let AI replace your own voice.

Practice solid communication skills consistently, and they—like your HMWK—will become second nature to you.

8

"Polite Confidence" Is the New PC

The phrase "politically correct" can be viewed as negative or positive, depending on the user and recipient of this description. In this book, PC is about the polite manner in which you exude confidence. Confidence continues to build throughout your career based on what you say and do and the outcomes (or consequences) thereof. This chapter offers some thoughts on how to display *polite confidence* in the workplace.

☐ **Bring your genuine enthusiasm, fresh ideas, and thoughtful mindset to the table.**

You weren't hired just because you had good grades. Your employer saw something in you that would fit with the organization and help it thrive. Be creative and express your ideas.

But keep in mind you also need to follow directions. If you think there may be a better way to complete a project that differs from your boss's instructions, check in with them first. You may not see the pitfalls of your new idea or know that your idea has already been tried and failed. You may even hear "If it ain't broke, don't fix it" if your boss doesn't have the time to contemplate the potential success of the new idea. Thank them for listening to your idea, and use the instructions you were given. Then again, your boss may love the idea and tell you to run with it!

Additionally, you may notice a recurring inefficiency in the workplace, and you have some ideas on how to fix it. Discuss the issue with your manager, and volunteer to spearhead an analysis of potential solutions, which may also include an estimate of time and costs saved. Your ingenuity, preparation, and professionalism will impress your manager, and you'll be viewed as someone who took ownership and genuinely cared about the success of the organization.

Don't be discouraged if any of your ideas are shot down. Remember, you are a newbie and should not confuse enthusiasm with wisdom. Despite the outcome, presenting the idea to your boss shows you take initiative and aren't afraid to express your idea in a respectful and confident manner.

You have to put yourself out there, and in so doing, you'll become more confident over time.

☐ **Ask and answer lots of questions.**

One of the biggest fears I had to overcome when I started my career was the idea that asking a question in the workplace, or answering one incorrectly, would make me look inexperienced or, even worse, dumb. This fear is perfectly natural, because you've just entered a new world where everyone seems to know more than you do. But, remember, much of their knowledge comes from years of experience, which you will gain in due time, and if you can muster the courage to ask and answer questions without fear, you'll actually display confidence.

It is OK to tell your boss you don't know the answer to their question. You are learning, and you're not expected to know all the answers. If you pretend to know, you will look ridiculous. It's better to promptly respond with an "I don't know" and then follow it up with an assurance that you'll do some research and get back to your boss as soon as possible with an answer. Then, of course, you need to actually do that in a timely manner.

It is *not* OK to say to your boss, "I know this is a dumb question, but . . ." Again, you are learning, so you're expected to ask lots of questions. Remember, your boss was once younger like you, and they understand that you will have questions and make mistakes. However, what is also crucial is that, before ever asking a question, you do everything possible to answer your question on your own within a reasonable amount of time. Research the problem. Determine alternative solutions. And then select the best one to present to your boss. Even if your selection is incorrect, it shows that you've taken initiative and demonstrated resourcefulness to find answers on your own.

Are you still afraid that you'll stumble along the way? You probably will! But you have to put yourself out there, and in so doing, you'll become more confident over time. Before you know it, the newbies will be asking *you* questions!

☐ **Set high standards and goals for yourself regardless of your peers' behavior.**
Standards and goals are not just about your quantitative performance but also involve the manner in which you achieve them. Disregarding standards or meeting targets by cutting corners may deliver short-term success, but it damages your credibility in the long run. Consistently respecting workplace standards and achieving workplace goals with honesty and respect shows maturity and earns lasting trust from your boss and colleagues.

Standards provide common benchmarks and define clear expectations. Your organization may have a standard requiring that employees arrive on time by 8:00 a.m. each day. That seems simple enough, but do you arrive ready for work by 8:00 a.m. each day, which takes us back to points in chapters 2 and 3 about coming to work ready to work? Similarly, you may observe that some of your coworkers are arriving consistently late or spending forty-five minutes eating their breakfast and putting on makeup at their desk. Shouldn't you be allowed to do the same? The answer is *Hell no!* (It's OK to curse here in your mind, not out loud.) You must hold yourself to a high standard regardless of what your peers are doing. It may seem unfair at the time, but you have to believe that your consistent appropriate behavior does not go unnoticed.

Goals serve as a road map for achieving desired results. Let's say your boss has a goal of completing the quarterly project two weeks ahead of schedule. Your first thought may be to remove certain parts of the process to save time. But the real goal is to complete the quarterly project two weeks ahead of schedule without compromising quality. That's a challenge that may require longer hours and working weekends in a shorter time span without any overtime pay. Do you complain about it to your boss, as your coworkers are doing? Or do you enthusiastically say, "I'm in. When do we start?!" The latter reaction underscores your commitment to the company goals. It also signals that you have confidence that the ambitious goal can be met.

Managers will have meetings about raises, bonuses, promotions, and terminations in which they openly discuss the quantitative performance of each employee. In some cases, the managers must fight for the furtherance of their department's employees by presenting the performance differences compared to their peers. When it's time for your performance review, you'll want to be seen by all the managers as someone who arrives on time ready to work, is willing to put in extra hours, strives to meet deadlines and other goals without compromising quality, and exhibits an air of confidence in addition to the other HMWK attributes.

☐ **Be yourself, your *professional* self.**
Being yourself at work requires confidence. But this means exercising good judgment and exhibiting *polite* confidence, not necessarily being your *entire* self at work. As we've already discussed, the workplace is not where you are free to express your opinions, beliefs, and emotions openly or to express your unique identity through your words, clothing, or social media presence. In the workplace, exhibiting polite confidence means knowing how and when to filter your speech and behavior, maintain composure, and show respect for all viewpoints.

Ultimately, professionalism is not about suppressing who you are but about presenting the best version of yourself as someone who wants to contribute their best to the workplace. You can still be authentic, but within the boundaries of respect and discretion. Over time, you will learn how to discern between what's appropriate in the professional and personal settings, and your professional self will become a refined extension of your personal self: thoughtful, self-aware, adaptable, and able to exercise good judgment and grace under pressure.

Professionalism is not about suppressing who you are but about presenting the best version of yourself as someone who wants to contribute their best to the workplace.

Key Points

Confidence in the workplace grows through your actions, communication, and integrity. Bring enthusiasm and fresh ideas to demonstrate your work ethic, but always show respect for your boss's direction and the organization's goals.

Ask and answer questions confidently, but with an appropriate degree of humility and manners.

Set and maintain high personal and professional standards for getting your work done and for how you achieve your goals.

In the workplace, being yourself means exercising good judgment, filtering speech and behavior when appropriate, and presenting the best version of who you are—authentic yet appropriate, confident yet considerate—so you can build trust and succeed without crossing workplace boundaries.

PART THREE

The Last Impression

9

Leave in a Blaze of Glory

You may be asking yourself, *Why is there a chapter on leaving my job when this book is about starting my job?* That's a fair question. Throughout the book you've been given tons of suggestions on how to make a great first impression, build credibility, and become indispensable in your new workplace. But no matter how much you love your job or how loyal you are to your employer, rarely would you work at your first career job your entire life. You never know when you may leave your organization; you might be moving, maybe you found a better job or were laid off or fired. How you handle that transition will speak volumes about your professionalism. Leaving gracefully can protect your reputation, preserve valuable relationships, and even open doors to future opportunities. In fact, the way you exit may be the last impression your boss and coworkers remember most.

Every effort you make today quietly shapes the opportunities that await you tomorrow.

Years ago, I joined two partners to begin a new family office and CPA firm. One of the young staff accountants working at the firm was also attending the local university to get her bachelor's degree in accounting. She was every company's dream employee and had the HMWK of a hundred employees. The partnership didn't work out for me, so I eventually decided to leave the firm. On my last day, I called her into my office and asked her to close the door. I wanted her to know how much I'd enjoyed working with her and how incredible she was at her job and as a person. I told her that one day she would leave the firm to pursue better opportunities, and, when she did, she should be sure to contact me so that I could be one of her references.

Five years later, I received a call from her telling me she was leaving the firm, and when she asked me to be one of her references, I was honored and wholeheartedly agreed. A few weeks later, I received a phone call from a manager at a very large local organization with whom she was interviewing. I provided a glowing reference, one of many, I'm sure, and she got the job. Ten years later, she is an Associate Vice President and the Controller of one of the largest public universities in the nation, after having earned her CPA, MBA, and other industry certifications along the way.

Her journey shows that hard work and integrity don't go unnoticed. She built her reputation one deadline, one project, and one act of professionalism at a time. Years later, those same qualities—and the people who witnessed them—became her greatest references. It's a reminder that every effort you make today quietly shapes the opportunities that await you tomorrow.

☐ **Don't be a "lame duck" in your final days.**
Your parting words and actions may be the last behaviors remembered about you. Finish all your work to the best of your ability. Teach others your job. Forward work papers and information to the appropriate colleagues. Provide an update on any projects you are handing over. Whatever it takes to help the company and your colleagues, work hard until the very last moment.

☐ **Don't burn bridges.**
You may feel like telling your boss or that horrible co-worker of the past five years to *Get lost!* This is definitely ill-advised. You are above that. You are a professional who has worked hard to practice HMWK, and you

should assume that, somehow and somewhere, any other type of behavior will come back to haunt you.

☐ **Thank everyone, personally, for how they've helped you in the job.**
Gather contact information that you may use later in your career. Stay in touch with people once you move on as part of your networking practice and maintain relationships with those people who may someday serve as references and will tout your professionalism.

Even if the job you're leaving wasn't your dream job, gather your positive takeaways and move on.

Key Points

Learning how to *leave a job gracefully* is just as important as starting one well. No matter how much you enjoy your first position, career changes are inevitable, whether by choice or circumstance. How you handle your exit reflects your professionalism and can influence future opportunities, as good manners and a continuing work ethic are often noticed most at the time of an employee departure. When leaving a job, always finish strong, stay professional, and express gratitude.

Your final impression may be the one that lasts.

Author's Note

Thank you for taking the time to read *The Graduate's Guide to Grace in the Workplace*. I sincerely hope that I have provided an abundance of useful insights to help you begin your new job. In my opinion, the most important takeaway from this book is this: A clear difference exists between the behavior in your professional life and your personal life, but success in both is a direct function of your HMWK and your application of the advice in *The Graduate's Guide*.

Sure, overlap will occur. It shows humility to say "I'm sorry" to a colleague (or a friend). It shows good manners when you open the door for your coworker (or your mom). It shows a strong work ethic when you work over the weekend to finish a company project (or to help your sister finish a personal project). It shows kindness when you attend the funeral of your boss's parent (or your best friend's parent). When you practice humility, good manners, strong work ethic, and kindness consistently, they become part of who you are, not just how you act from nine to five.

As I said earlier in the "Letter to the Reader," now is the time to become the person you choose to be. You were taught humility, good manners, a strong work ethic, and kindness throughout your life from various people, but it's possible you haven't actually *applied* those lessons in everyday life as well as you could. The good news is that you have the power to change that—starting right now.

And I know you can do it.

Very truly yours,
Aunt Anna

Notes

1. US Department of Education, National Center for Education Statistics (NCES). *Digest of Education Statistics, 2023*. Table 318.10, "Degrees Conferred by Postsecondary Institutions, by Level of Degree and Sex of Student: Selected Years, 1869–70 through 2031–32." NCES, October 2023, https://nces.ed.gov/programs /digest/d23/tables/dt23_318.10.asp. Postsecondary includes four-year, two-year, and less-than-two-year (i.e., occupational and vocational) schools as defined in NCES Appendix B Glossary.

2. Carnegie, Dale. *How to Win Friends & Influence People.* Simon & Schuster, 1936.

3. Although this saying is widely attributed to Benjamin Franklin (1706–90), no definitive record of its use by him exists.

4. Although often attributed to Socrates (470–399 BCE), there is no historical evidence that he ever said it. The earliest known version of this quote appears in *The Eleanor Roosevelt Papers* (Franklin D. Roosevelt Library, Hyde Park, New York), where Eleanor

Roosevelt is credited with writing: "Great minds discuss ideas; average minds discuss events; small minds discuss people."

5. Although this quotation is commonly attributed to Albert Einstein (1879–1955), no definitive primary source has been found.

6. Cutlip, Scott M., and Allen H. Center. *Effective Public Relations*. 1st ed. Prentice-Hall, 1952.

7. Google. "Guide: Understand Team Effectiveness (Project Aristotle)." re:Work. https://rework.withgoogle.com/intl/en/guides/understanding-team-effectiveness/.

Acknowledgments

I thank God for all He has given me.

About the Author

Anna Pikounis Paine, MAcc, CPA, has more than thirty years of experience navigating diverse corporate settings. She leads her own CPA firm, offering outsourced CFO and controller services to small- and medium-sized businesses as well as to high-net-worth clients in Palm Beach County, Florida. Her clients have spanned industries, from finance to automotive to real estate to law. In addition to her accounting practice, Anna has served as an Adjunct Professor of Accounting Technology at Indian River State College. She received her Master of Accounting degree from the University of Florida and undergraduate degrees in finance from the University of Florida and accounting from the University of South Florida. She lives in Jupiter, Florida, with her husband and has two sons who are now navigating the workplace as emerging professionals—experiences that inspire her commitment to guiding the young generation through *The Graduate's Guide to Grace in the Workplace.*

www.ingramcontent.com/pod-product-compliance
Lightning Source LLC
Chambersburg PA
CBHW070613170726

48004CB00018B/1304